A Matriarch's Song

Poems by Betty Lockwood

Peter E. Randall
Publisher
Portsmouth, New Hampshire
2001

Special thanks to Margaret Robinson and Susan Wyant for their help in bringing this book to its completion

Cover photograph by Margaret Robison.

© 2001 by Betty Lockwood
Printed in the United States of America

Additional copies available from the author at
79 Warner Hill Road, Charlmont, MA 01339

Peter E. Randall Publisher
Box 4726, Portsmouth, NH 03802

Contents

Acknowledgments	6
Untitled	7
Song of the Matriarch	8
Gathering	9
Playing the Chances	10
A Traveling Story	11
Morning Love Song	12
Advice	13
Duality	15
Random Thoughts on Starting a Day	16
Blessing	17
A Cat and a Fire and a Winter Night	18
Autumn	19
Death	20
Despair	21
Lullaby	22
Initiation	23
Touch	24
Traveling	25
Anyway	26
Say Thank You	27
Dance the Circle	28
3 A. M.	30
Learning	31
Taboo	32
Bon Voyage to Myself	33
On The Road	34
Keeping On	35
Surviving	36
Another Day Begins	37
Day Break	38
Bed Time	39
Passion	40
Transit	41

THE ROUND SOUND OF JOY	42
EIGHTY-FIVE	43
I WANNA DANCE I WANNA RUN	44
WHEN I WAS YOUNG	45
LEAVING STAR ISLAND AND ON A WINTER DAY REMEMBERING	46
MISC.	48
OLD SENSUALIST	49
SECOND GROWTH	50
SIMPLE WORDS	51
A MESSAGE	52
GRIEF	53
UNTITLED	54
UNTITLED	55
UNTITLED	56
AS I SHALL EVER BE	57
TO OUR BODIES	58
BLESSINGS AND HARMONIES	59
NUANCES OF INTIMACY	60
LOVE LETTER	61
CASTING BACK	62

Acknowledgments

This is not a one-person book. It is the result of the inspiration, interest, encouragement, and help of many writers, readers, and friends. I thank all of you.

Since my first reading at the Arms Library in Shelburne Falls, people have expressed genuine interest in what I've read and said. And I've been enriched by hearing the wide assortment of work by other writers who have read there.

I also met a rich variety of writers in one of Gene Zeiger's workshops, a workshop, which I attended as long as I was able to get there. I'm grateful to Gene not only for support of my writing, but for introducing me to the poetry of Anna Akhmatova.

Pru Grand took me with her to a private workshop, a small group of women writing together and responding to each other's poetry. They asked me to join them. I've been a part of that group for about six years. One day I told them I wanted to gather some of my poems together in a book. Everyone—Pru, Elisabeth Leete, Susie Patlove, Linda Putnam, Juliet Seaver, and Bonnie Wodin—all immediately jumped in and began to talk about it. The poems were in a notebook with me and the women divided them up that day and took them home to read. Their generosity was unlimited. My gratitude to them is also unlimited. My gratitude is unlimited also to Susan Wyant for her work on the book. And to Margaret Robison, who has played such an important role in my life, and in the completion of this work.

I want to thank my daughter Clarise for her enduring love and support.

The night is full of
The spilling of dreams of myself
My self remembers my self
The self spilling all of itself back
into itself
The self never grows into more
My self remembers always
My self will remember when it spills
Itself that it is in a place where
it has always belonged

Song of the Matriarch

I said yes.
Then I knew.
Then I lived,
had sons and daughters
They lived. Said yes.
Had sons and daughters
who have sons and daughters.
Is it only so I may know
there will be more
who know what yes is
that I am made rich with time?
Does time need us to measure itself?
Now time needs me to say
yes to its embraces; needs me
to spawn words and spread
them as I have sown seeds.

I will not sit and wait.
I will go into the water.
I will go into the fire.
I will drink the fire and be fed.
I will be charred by the water.
Nothing has only one face.

Say yes.

Gathering

Here is family gathered.
Here is kinship accepted.
For all the caring we can
give one another,
For all the sharing we can do,
For all the giving we do
with generous hearts,
For all the receiving we
do with graciousness,
Let us bless each other;
Let us be good to each other;
And let us enjoy,
oh do let us enjoy
our time together.

May love and memories linger.

Dedicated to my kin

Playing the Chances

Let me, in fancy, enter the womb again
take that precipitant plunge into life
one particular sperm, one particular egg
one chance, one blind collision—

Let me be that minute explosion
of life creating itself,
let me know womb and water and warmth
and dark and swimming and growing
and infant born.

Let me become—cell by cell, division by
division, moving moving becoming more
inexorable growing destined for the
mountain shaking earth birthing day.

From one spasmodic incident
from minute speck of egg and sperm
with urgency to grow
and here am I

still becoming me—growing
still becoming me dying
passing life on through me

O let me in fancy enter the womb again
and for an instant taste life emergent
coming through playing the chances.

A Traveling Story

I remember mother when I, a small child
would seek her lap as she rested, rocking
in a chair, till chores and conscience
pestering, she'd slap her thigh, and call
a sharp command: "Come on legs!"
A whining voice, surely not her own,
would issue whimpering "No. No. Let us rest"
A few more minutes we'd rock and then once
more: "Come on legs!" And cuffing the leg,
she'd rise, dump me back to my own activity
and face the continent of her life again.
She walked it every day, happy days or
hurting days, making her own paths.

Now I chronicle my living, become my own
cartographer, map my unique geography.
Here an isthmus wind whipped and wild seas.
When sights are desolate, no direction seems
a likely one for path breaking, and I fear to
turn an ankle, take a fall, know only reluctance,
I stop, put up a fence, and sit, wondering
briefly is this tragedy or petulance or wise
self sufficiency, and I remember mother
"Come on Legs!"

Morning Love Song

Leaping this morning
from sleep
to wide awake
to loving,
smiling and stretching
in my old body,
in my single bed,
I heard happiness singing
come aboard, come aboard,

I said hello to the morning
that sat outside the window in the dark
waiting for the sun to come
and say, okay, it is time to become today.
I said good-bye to the night
which had cradled me in the darkness.

I heard my breath and then I felt it
going in and out of my body,
and it was barely whispering,
but its song was *stay alive, stay alive.*
And the heart kept repeating
in a sort of spasm of being,
one more beat, one more beat.
Jointed bones, cautiously
testing themselves,
tentative—then with assurance—
we can, we can.

I waited in bed for the light
to breach the windows
and come into the room
and find me
and this old body
singing as if its success in being

awake once more
was a triumph:
as if I was not just one,
but a troupe—
performers waiting to go forth
dancing and singing
along with the trumpeting of the day
announcing itself.

I waited in the bed.
The day declared itself.
The body declared itself.
They said hello.
Legs and hips
        lifted me
                out of the bed,
and love
     whirled along
            in a dance
                  and sang.

Advice

When you wake to the day
with the accumulation
of years lying upon you,
the trash bin of a life
spreads out as far as
recollection takes you—
treasures and trash
nothing recyclable
stories grown moldy
music discordant
muscles and bones and memories
all thinning, weakening—

Then leave the bed
shake out your body,
shake out your life—
clean yourself
brush and shine yourself
tie bright ribbons on yourself
put dangles in your ears say to the clock "strike the hour"
say to the flutes "make music"
say to the sun "stay awhile"
say to the body "ready or not!"
and to the day "here I come!"

Walk out from the catch all
rooms of your sleep.

Duality

A.M. Up. Standing by the bed,
body in whining rebellion,
hurting, demanding to be fed.

There's food to fix—clothes to don—
teeth to brush—legs to walk—
dishes to wash—birds to feed—
letters to write—talk to talk—
bills to pay—books to read—

When suddenly
the crazy little old lady
who lives in the mirror
that hangs on the back
of my bedroom door,
said "To hell with the whole shebang
today!" and let out a merry roar.
"What fun to be eighty and one
and a crazy old lady to boot.
Stay long in your bed,
or up with the sun;
no one but you gives a hoot!"

She whispered a titter,
and grinned a revolt.
"There is no one
but our very own selves
who can
boss ourselves around!"

Random Thoughts on Starting a Day

1
Awake, I draw breath.
Before the exhalation
is complete, I live.

2
Steeping in sun's warmth,
murmuring with gratitude,
hold, heal, I still am.

3
Old age makes the bed
trusting that a smooth top sheet
conceals the wrinkles.

4
Solitude is a
garment, retailored to my
measure everyday.

5
Old age is not so
bad, you know? And talking to
yourself is okay.

6
One day breath will stop;
eternity will greet me
ticking my last tock.

Blessing

Birch bark, shell of the fallen tree,
torn into small strips,
too incendiary for casual use,
are fed piece by tattered piece
to the pocket of heat the stove holds.
Reminders of the tree once living
drawn into flame the warmth from
any remainders of last night's fire.
For another morning, flame and I
deny death.

Rising—heat from the sequestered
cache of coals
is surely nature's grace bestowed.
Let all simple gifts
be recognized and named,
thanked for being,
handled with care,
accepted with grace,
remembered.

A Cat and a Fire and a Winter Night

Late in the cold night, in flannel gown
and slippered feet, I stood before
the open stove, feeding strips of bark
to hot ash, warily watching for
ash to become glow and glow become flame.

Suddenly—what was it? No sound, no
movement, yet I turned to the glass
paned door and found wide amber eyes
locked upon me, saw myself reflected,
and at my mirrored feet
great yellow cat, seated, staring
no fur rose, no eye blinked,
no twitch of tail spoke awareness.
What was real? What was figment?

Witch cat, wanderer of the woods,
night hunter, survivor of any weather,
what brought you up the hill,
out of the snow hushed woods,
choosing your path through the trees—
to this door, to watch a maker of fire?
Observing? Curious only—or lending power?
What stiffened me, held me, fire
forsaken, watching your eyes?
What sense of kin trembled? What memory
lurked in our curious yearnings?

Was it the moon that moved, barely sliding
in the sky—or was it a cloud slipping past?
I reclaimed my eyes, broke the spell,
laid the log, set the draft, took the light,
let darkness have the house, left you to your wanderings.

I would not have opened the door had you asked.
You would not have entered if I had.

Autumn

Jennifer, the cat, has died where
she lay in the sunlight, curled
up in her pied colored coat.

No more dainty acceptance
from my hand of a bite
of cheese, her rough tongue
lingering for the last savory
taste on my fingers.

No more wide open mouthed
entreaties for entrance
when a day turns wet or cold,
resonating cries dumbed out by
windowed door to silent pleas
passionate in mime.

No more impressive arrangements of
muscles grown old, positioned for
meticulous tongue lapping as she
groomed in her silken entirety . . .
all clean, smooth, all properly done.

Neither owned or owning except
as friends who shared
this porch and stair,
she is missed, calico cat, curled
up in her aging beauty
where she gently died alone.

Death

Don't linger at my chimney
or come cracking my door open,
peeking in.
Don't lay your ear on my chest
or touch me with those
stethoscopic fingers.
This heart is still working.
Just leave it alone.

Oh, it was nice of you to stop
and inquire;
but don't you have other calls
to make today?

No, don't worry about me.
Take your time;
take your time.
I'm in no hurry.
I'll be patient.
I'll wait for you.

Despair

When did living become old age?
When did dailiness become another year past?

When did pain become an anchor
holding the craft in the shallows
tangled in the weeds of the sea?
When did rudder become useless,
currents take control?

When did waking in the pathless dark
become fearful, tangled quilts
become chains holding you down?
When did bruise become fatal injury,
and dry eyed crying begin?

When did dying become safer than living,
fasting more to the taste than savories?

When did living begin to be suicide?
Waking a noose?
Sunlight a lie?

LULLABY

Listen:
I don't mind growing old; it's just
not wanting to become weak, tired,
waiting with boredom for death. I want
to go on being, not gone forever, till
all who knew me are not here anymore to
even remember I once was.
I don't want it to be over with.
I don't want to ever stop wanting to be,
to be me, in love with myself,
hunger and habit driven, taking nourishment
from life, denying transience.
I open my throat and howl
"Not ready, not ready," spewing
a barrier of noise, a fence of sound
around the mortal self—
But wait   Hush   Stand silent   Chided
This old body knows death is in the house;
death is sleeping in these bones.
So   hush   Hush
Live well in this 'brief everlasting—
Grief, too, will be ever passing—

INITIATION

As a small child, I learned
rolling down hill with others,
bodies bumping, atop, beneath,
close as possible, breathless
with abandonment, running
up to another rolling feast,
was a very secret never
failing trembling delight.

As ten year olds, Martha and I relished
the occasional sleeping over, when presumed
to be asleep, we read by flashlight, and as
curious eager explorers, cuddled and tickled,
fondled with awe and excitement while pleasure
for which we had no name, grew in the loins and
snaked through the body. Martha showed me how
to do it to myself with the eraser end of a
pencil. Crude technique, but sophisticated knowledge
that body could be pleasured anytime, at your own will.

Now, when edgy with desire,
I think of Martha, little
hedonist who taught me true;
and mother, shamed and shaming,
who told me lies. Living truth,
forgiving lies, knowing my years
to be long, and more to come,
I caress myself.

Touch

Reaching out of a hand
brush of fingers against cheek

sudden hug holding you
whisper of lips to lips
feel of flesh against flesh—
The body speaks so many ways.

No cat, no dog do I seek
for tactile comfort.
It's human flesh alone that
speaks a language I understand.

When I am dying, if any
is with me, please touch me.
Whoever you are, open the palm
of your hand to my cheek.
Let me die being touched
by human hands ungloved.

TRAVELING

All it takes is being very quiet
and remembering.
The words are "Live. Live. Live."
The other words are "Death will come"
"Be patient." "Let it happen"
Say "Once upon a time."
Smile at your memories.

Look outside. Look inside.
Both views belong to you.
Infant. Crone. Companions now
One remembering.
One saying farewell.
Traveling well together.

Anyway

There are times when the pain you say isn't here,
comes anyway. Proving only that wearing out
will not heal. Rust conquers oil, coats of paint,
and digests the metal—anyway!
All of that is true, and mumbling about
it won't become poetry. Not anyway!
But anyway, here I am, inevitably, even
contentedly, moving along to the recycling
center, to wait my turn, singing a
traveling song.

Let's whistle while we rust
Drink nourishment from dust—
Acknowledge that we must—

And follow the yellow brick road,
Hi Ho Hi Ho Hi Ho—
Anyway!

Say Thank You

When I wake each day in silence
and hear inside myself, "Oh, good morning,
good morning, darling,"
it's life itself I greet, and me alive.
The day and I salute each other, not
promising anything; just saying
hello, just saying, I'm ready.

Words shake free of sleep
and call to the day, to
the sun that comes, to
the heart that beats, to
the body ready to accept itself.

I anthropomorphize the sunlight,
the turn of the planet, the machinery
of the universe. I throw forth
morning celebrations,
and prayers for the day,

for life has called my name again
and I'm responding to it.
Say joy, say life, say
breathe in and breathe out,
say thank you.

Dance the Circle

Ring around the rosey, a pocket full of posey,
Ashes, ashes, all fall down.

A song's asinging, wanting to be born,
kicking, pushing, trying to be born—
Come, come, we'll all sing together,
sing the birthing song,
round and round, fall down, fall down,
laugh, scramble to your feet,
start all over again.

Ring around the rosey rosey rosey
pocket full of posey posey posey

Old lady, you can't fall down and play;
you'll lie there and hurt—
Yes I can—yes I can—dance the ring
dance the ring, pocket full of posies,
toss the petals, whirl the skirt,
stamp your feet, click-clack the floor,
feel the beat—stamp the beat—
skip, skip, run, catch the others, hold hands, hold hands
all of you, reach for the hands,
cling, hold and cling, together together sing sing
Sing your breath gone.
Hold me, lean away, balance, whirl, sing,
dance dance dance the circle—

Of children there are five—
grandchildren there are seven—
children's children's children
and more a coming on—more a coming on—
How many are we to dance—say a number—
a magic number a wisdom number a mystery and a message number
join us, join us, —come and count yourselves, say yourselves,

name yourselves, place yourselves, —circle circle circle we all belong—
Some are angry, some are dead, some don't want to play—
mother, come and play.

Hold the circle, whirl the circle, hold the shape,
tumble now, sprawl now, scramble now, let go.
Laugh laugh laugh reach for hands reach for laughter—
all falldown falldown falldown—

We left out the ashes, we forgot the ashes,
ashes in the bones
and the clocks running down.

Sing oh sing oh sing the day.
hold oh hold and swing the day—
Dance the circle, wind the wheels—
click-clack, don't look back,
tick-tock forget the clock.

I'll paint the picture, I'll write the music,
I'll hold your hands.
ringaround ringaround ringaround—

My turn to be the ashes—
My turn to be the dust—
circle circle whirl the circle
dance dance dance hold hands
giggle, squirm, laugh laugh sing
sing my breath away,
sing the circle sing the dance—

Stamp the feet, stamp the beat, ratatat ratatat
toss the head—leap—reach for air—
reach for hands reaching for air—
cling hold now faster faster faster
ring around the rosey laughter laughter laughter

Ashes—Ashes—all fall down....

3 A. M.

Persuaded that if I say there is
no pain, there is no pain,
I thought to rule my life:

growing old with painless ease,
remembering with no regrets,
being alive always enough,

fears conquered and dispersed
before they burrowed
and made nests.

Now I cannot rout them out—
not the pain, not the
sorrows, not the fears.

Yet here I am, still avid, a tick
clamping into any flesh it finds,
sucking my sustenance as I must,

convinced this midnight's dampened breath
will quickly freshen as the sun rises,
that low tides turn, and turning, sing.

Dedicated to Clarise Patton

LEARNING

I would be your mother, your child,
your lover, your friend,
your judge, your defender,
your student, your teacher,
proud beside you, humble beside you.

Can my words outline you?
Can my hopes define you?

I am learning love.
I am learning you.

Taboo

No, you cannot,
You are too young.
Because I say so.
Do what I tell you to do.
Don't touch.
Don't let anyone touch you.
Don't say that word.
Where did you learn it?
What will others think?
Why can't you be—?
You should be ashamed of yourself.

Taboo was my mother.
Taboo was my teacher.
Taboo was my jailer.
But taboo was never my playmate.

And now old age has thumbed her nose
and chased taboo away,
cut off her corsets,
dances nude,
Just for the fun of it.

Bon Voyage to Myself

Take life easy
take life slow
Don't decide ahead of time
Where it is you want to go.

Around this corner
Or the next
Life may simplify itself
Or become damned complex.

And so I live, so I live
And probably shall, till Death
and I rendezvous ahead
Beside the roadway marker:

"Zone Of Final Breath"

On The Road

Yeah, I'm on the road
scared a bit sometimes

sort of lost, sort

of wandering around;
but I ain't lonely,
I tell you that.
I got friends
to travel with;
we've got talking to do
we've got plans to make.
So get away from me
Mr. Death Mr. Death
I ain't going no place
with you yet.
No way am I agoing
with you yet.

Yeah, scared a bit
but finding my way.
I'm still on the road,
not turning back;
So you get away from me now
Old mister Death.

It's going to be a good day, friends,
You and me traveling together
laughing on the way and loving
the journey and each other.

Keeping On

My miserable leg and my mended leg are partners.

My vanity was my legs, shapely, slim but sturdy
soft white skin that tanned to bronze.
Those and my blond hair were self
approval badges; chamomile rinses
with every shampoo, slow loving brushings.
In study hall choose a seat where the sun
will highlight your golden hair.

Now, with every grooming, hair comes out in a mix
of muddy brown and gray, and legs, purpled with
twisted veins and swollen knees, demanding
cane assistance, cane reliance.

But stronger than vanity is my passion for them.
Constant as my breath is gratefulness.
Conversing with them, massaging and oiling them,
I tell them my admiration for their endurance.

Then call them out!
Still places to go.
Tell them please
keep on keeping on.

Surviving

Okay, woman,
lying here grieving,
tasting tears;
blow your nose;
get out of bed.
Resume yourself.
Pattern the day.

Remember.
Remember with love.
Dance jigs of joy
in your versatile
imagination.
Sing love songs,
even if off-key.

Memorize living.
Morning pills,
3 with a glass of water.

Vision new scenes.
Rehearse laughing.
The curtain stays up.
You're still on stage.

Another Day Begins

I get out of bed, stand on my feet,
test knees with shallow bending.
I tell legs I will appreciate
their walking my body
to the bathroom.
They whine about doing all the work.

Head grumbles,
says I am spoiling
the cry baby legs.
It is their *duty* to walk.

Torso has listened.
Impatient, it speaks out.
"Hey!
I must go to the toilet
or I will pee on
those whining legs!
I must have food in the stomach
or I'll give that arrogant head
a huge pain."

Bickering, they hold me captive
while they negotiate.

Oh, I love this stupid body.
Pretty soon we all begin
to laugh together
while I clean the teeth
that have languished at ease
all night, in a warm bath.

Where would we be without each other?

Let's sing: "Oh, we'll all go together
when we go————"

Daybreak

I sing the day into being
as the sun rises
to bless and warm,
to coax us from sleep,
to return us from fear,
to declare a day.

I sing the day to acknowledge pain,
to acknowledge love,
to declare myself,
to declare you.
This day shall be of song.

Bedtime

I fix the fire, adjust the draft for the night—
pour a glass of milk
and take a cookie—
But I'm telling you I love you,
and I'm laughing with you,
and I put my arms around you
and we dance around in a crazy circle.
Now I'm in bed with the milk and the cookie
and soon I'll be asleep.

What will I dream tonight?

Passion

Friends, are you prepared for this?
This passion of old age?
Are you ready to sip the rich broth
the simmering stock has become?
Enjoy the bewildering
wonder of the blend?
Taste of herbs casually added?
A bit more salt perhaps?
Some chili powder?
Go ahead. Experiment.
Enjoy.

Transit

All that is begun
first roots, then rots.
I stood before I walked.
Always becoming, I must learn
myself before I die.

I look now for wholeness.
In every waking
wonder at the partial self
left wandering in sleep.
Why am I not at home with myself?

Has age recast me, hidden
my intimate, dubbed me alien?
Old lady, find your infancy.
Recall your beginning.
Recognize your end.

Hold the sweet flesh close.
Stroke the wrinkled face.
All that was begun is leaving.
Flow denies stagnation.
Ebb greets it as they pass.

The Round Sound Of Joy

To my 10-month old grandson, on my 80th birthday

Rolling along the floor
one round baby, three balloons,
round and red and ribbon entwined,
and ricochets of rainbow light
bouncing from prisms and sun,
dancing the walls.
Reach, reach for it all.
It will not be caught.
will not be held.
Curling along the floor together,
round balloons on top of you,
under you, sliding away,
round baby, round balloons, round laughter
rolling through a world of round joy,
never trapped, never held.
Reach   touch   all bounces   slips away
and you on your round belly hitch along
crowing with bellowings of round laughter
and reach reach for the magic,
the magic that won't be caught.
All, all has a life of its own.

Eighty-Five

As I grow older, I feel younger
more eager, more full of love.
More alive the closer I move to death.
More whole the closer I move in to blight.
The sweeter life grows as fervent
clamors of youth pass.
Passions of old age take deeper
flavor, ripened, more nuanced.
More easily words and affections
flow when the self-conscious gaucherie
of youth has passed.

Wholeness suddenly is mine;
ragged edges of fear hemmed.

Mirrors say Look. Do not
be afraid. You are what you are.

I Wanna Dance, I Wanna Run

This body is nostalgic for suppleness and strength
remembering hand stands, turning cart wheels,
longing to move that way again—swift,
sure, precise and unafraid—
muscles tempted by body skills recalled

running, skating, energy and will,
short legs conquering the adult two wheeler-
the wonderful leaping pogo stick, up into the air,
again and again, up and down porch stairs .
Oh the body remembers well—

Scar on the shin remembers too
the edge of the concrete step, the bloody gash,
the long time healing.
Mind warns wait—wait—listen
to the muscles that grieve—

First thrust of the body
turning itself upside down
feet leaving the floor
hands grasping the floor
would end in disaster
a heap of twisted muscles
cracked bones
a pile of flesh
in pain disabled.

This body sighs, resigns itself, accepts.
Nostalgia whimpers.

When I Was Young

I was old knowing what it meant
to be lonesome when my sister died.

Old knowing some things can't be fixed.
A broken toy? "Daddy can't fix? Throw it away!"

Old knowing that keeping very quiet,
finding a dark space to crawl into, felt safe.

Old, knowing when someone tried to trick me
I could say my anger.

Two joints of a chicken wing
are not the same as a wishbone!

Now I am truly old; memories
find a way to creep into my sleep.
I hear the ghosts cry.

Leaving Star
and on a Winter Day Remembering

Yes, the sun still rises over East Rock,
still sets over Portsmouth Town.
Swallows return, nest under
Oceanic porch, and over the entrance door.

Milkweed still blossoms, offering
nectar for the Monarch butterflies,
and green leaves on which to lay the
eggs soon to change to green larva
on their way to becoming more of the same
chain, and fascinating to watch—

Of course the chapel on the hill
becomes aglow at night as lighted
candles are carried one by one
up the rocky hill and the bell is tolled.

Rocks still loom and
tidal pools form between them;
anemones still cling, feed
from every swell of water
entering—departing—flow
that never stills, that
cannot settle into stagnancy.

The wind still blows
the rocks still stand
the tides still flow
the birds still nest
milkweed still grows,
People remember
and are remembered

and the call "come back
come back" still sounds.

Misc.

What do the old old
do with memories?
Make a home for them
with words.

When dreams pass judgments
on you and ghosts cry
you have lost your way.
Wake up.

Grapes my own feet trod
made choicest wines.
Feet earned drunkenness.
I dance.

Trees turned red and gold
seek admiration.
Hemlocks wait for snow,
then shine.

OLD SENSUALIST

It happens. Growing old.
No doubt of that.

But becoming weak and
tired, anticipating death?

I don't want life to be over,
to stop wanting a part in it.
Am I in love with myself?
Or with the world?

Will having been be enough
when being has departed?
My non-self cannot answer,
having no memory of having been.

How unreal. I'll not be
able to remember myself!

Second Growth

What would I be
if you were not?
What my joy?
Where my genesis?

I asked: let me call you friend.
I did not know it would be like this.

With your gardener's easy way
of tending, I've been double dug;
clay and sand becoming
loam, fertile with compost,
sweet with lime,
friable.
Roots find deep paths
and share with earthworms.

Growing from once dormant soil
a strange abundance over-spills.
What seeds were tossed here
to bring such produce?

I tell you this is
a different garden now,
neither Eden nor farmland,
but small acreage bearing richly
in forgotten corners.

Dedicated to May Sarton

Simple Words

"My son is a builder."
I said the words;
You heard their poetry.
"I like the way that sounds;
listen to it."
You spoke simply, ear cocked
as if still listening.
Did you hear mother pride, mother love?
Hear hammer and saw at work?
Did you vision house
by plank and stud and rafter
rising till, roof in place
a fir bough is fastened to the ridge,
thanking the trees for lumber,
blessing the house?

This is thank you to a poet
who reminded me to listen to words
for the poetry just under their skin,
and taught me that simple words
can bear the weight of saying it whole.

Dedicated to May Sarton

A Message

There are words to be said today.
To write them on paper and trust
the postal service to take them to you
is not the way I would choose.
They will be words of love,
and words of love should be whispered.
They should be the first quick spontaneous
words of the morning,
murmured into your ear
to wake you with a slow smile,
to move you from sleep to wake
to remembering
that you were born in love,
fashioned by love,
grew with love, gave love, accepted love,
and still walk the earth loving and beloved,
and be glad this is so.

Dedicated to May Sarton

Grief

If you wish to talk to me
your voice must come through
the silence that is blotting me out.
Subtle words, softly spoken
even though wise
will not negotiate the shadows
of this silence.

I could suffocate here, in my living self,
in this house, this bed,
listening to the whispering of my breath
that, on automatic, still operates
in the name of living,
the first priority.

On May Sarton's death

I answer the phone. It is not your voice.
It is some other one. It is not you.
It is a comforter—tender—alive-loving
wanting to solace. It is not you.
Friends write me letters. They love me.
They want to hold me to the edge of life
where happiness is still operative.
They are ready to catch me if I stumble,
to lift me if I fall.
They have strong arms held out to me.
I love them.
They are not you.

Dedicated to May Sarton

Is this grief then—to destruct?
To think at night, "I managed today;
I'll be all right tomorrow?"
and then to wake in the morning, disarmed,
and know the soft rot advancing?

A banana, slowly, under its skin
grows soft. Brown speckled,
the skin retains the look
of an edible fruit for a long time
after the succulence collapses upon itself.

On May Sarton's death

Your time of flesh is over;
my time of flesh is still upon me.
Technically dead, and not yet dead
have melded.
You dead and myself stripped
to a grieving core, finding
no flesh upon my bones,
no bones to bear the non-flesh,
I laid my body full length and naked
beside your body full length and naked,
suckled each upon the breasts of the other.
We know without having learned.
We are without being alive.
Flowing into each other,
I dwell in your death;
you dwell in my life.

On May Sarton's death

As I Shall Ever Be

With you dead these many months
I had dreamed passions dried away,
Life winterbound forever.
Yet still I live warming
myself at that fire,
as I have ever been, shall ever be.

Branded with that hot iron
how indelible the marks I wear.
Tattoos of every shade, radiant,
will outlive the flesh itself.

Dedicated to May Sarton

To Our Bodies

Seized with tenderness, old lady,
I ache to love you,
You with body mutilated
In order to heal.
You said passion is over
When the blade takes

Sacrificed flesh.

I say our old bodies are soft
And beautiful.
Let softness seek softness.
Let caress be answered by caress.
Let scar meet scar.
Let love meet love.
Let fires burn.
We have years of kindling stored here.

I am seized with tenderness, old lady.
Let me kiss your scar.

Dedicated to May Sarton

Blessings and Harmonies

(for a friendship)

This was sudden and this was true.
This cannot be altered.
I am created in you and you in me
and each remains herself whole.
This is bread and milk.
This is roses and lilies
and violets and wild strawberries.
This is friend and friend and always so.

Space is there to keep you from being crowded.
Space is there to give you a place to go.
Space is there to hold quiet
and perhaps be shared.

Margaret—Elizabeth—the names are comfortable
with each other. The names are tokens.
They are not interchangeable.
Two separate bells, both ringing.

To Margaret Robison (1st poem)

Nuances of Intimacy

"The child climbs from her bed. She is
wearing cotton underpants and is barefooted"
from *The Naked Bear*
          by Margaret Robison

I sweep her up in my arms,
nuzzle pursed kissing lips
into her navel, making smacking sounds
while she laughs and squirms in the embrace,
her tender warm skin flushed.

I watched, briefly, hands fastening
brace to your bare leg, glanced
smooth skin, white, beautiful
soft nakedness. Struck sharply by desire
to lay hand on your flesh, a caress.
Knew fear of my tactile self.

You, being yourself, support me.
I, being myself, reach to heal you.
You, with wheelchair trailing, are walking.
I, with cane thumping, walking beside you.
Our caring invisible support,
each for the other, making
wheelchair and cane for the time being
invisible also? The two of us—a team—
alive to each other—loving—laughing—
walking—sharing—going along.

To Margaret Robison

LOVE LETTER

Most beautiful, most loved, most gracious,
let the words flow out and surround you.
A curtain lifted and I saw you.
A curtain lifted and I went to you.
A curtain lifted, never to be lowered.
Look up and see all space.
Look around and see all beauty.
Look around and see all life.
Years are tramping along,
step after step, after step,
keeping the rhythm.
Do not fall. You know the march.
The beat is in you.
You live most completely,
reaching into every corner,
knowing the dark holes,
knowing the sunlit rooms.
Most beautiful, most gracious,
most loved.

To Margaret Robison,
written sometime during the night of her birthday, November 7

Casting Back

Where will I walk today,
with the small bells ringing, calling
my feet to follow.
Where will I find the little lost paths?
Do they rise from sleep and dreams,
or only lead back to that nocturnal place?

Where is the hillside covered with violets?
A small girl picked a bouquet for you.

Where is the sunset mauve and pink and streaked
with sunlight still as it purpled into night?
And where is the storm that followed?

Where is the little girl I keep
trying to save from drowning?